Pickleball For Beginners Exercises

Maximize Your Potential in Pickleball by Unlocking the Power of Pre-Game Rituals and Post-Game Recovery Techniques for Peak Performance(Illustrated Exercises)

Dennis Hall

Contents

References

Introduction

This guide is collectively beneficial for the players of every level to prepare their bodies to make them more flexible for an intense game.

Pickleball has gained popularity in the past few years as a sport and a fun outdoor activity. No matter if you are a seasoned player or playing, get started with pickleball.

However, the key to mastering your game in both scenarios is ***warming up your body*** properly to lose the stiffness and stress to give your hundred percent. This surely helps in improving performance and prevents injuries.

From dynamic stretching exercises to ball handling drills, we have tried to compile tailored pickleball warm-up exercises for kids/adults and older people, along with benefits, in order to create an effective routine to meet the physical demands of pickleball.

However, you must be careful and particular according to your age and the intensity of your warm-ups, as they are more likely to increase your heart rate.

This guide has been specifically compiled for the champs to warm up their muscles effectively and improve their agility and footwork through various fun, engaging warm-up exercises and their cooldowns to bring it back to normal.

Chapter One

Pickleball Warm-Up and Cool Down for Ultimate Performance

What are warm-up and cool-down?

W arm-up is a physical activity for the whole body with a gradual increase in intensity. At the same time, the cool-down is more like regulating the pulse to the regular heart rate.

Regarding pickleball, unlikely tennis or badminton, it requires more active body movement and warm-up before the game helps to stretch the body without sore-ness—preparing your body for the tournament.

Types of Warm-ups

Warm-ups of every kind ease the workout and minimize the internal viscosity of muscles to cope effectively during intense stress.

There are a lot of different injury-free warm-up sets, but usually, they are categorized into three main techniques, which include *cardio, dynamic, and static stretches.*

1. Cardio Warm-Up

The cardio warmup improves blood flow and increases the body temperature. The typical cardio warmups are

- *Jogging*

- *Butt kickers and high knees*

- *Jumping ropes, and*

- *Mountain climbers*

These warmups help prepare your body for normal to intense physical activities.

1. Dynamic

The dynamic style warmup helps to open your joints and muscles, which allows your body to open to the full range of dynamic bodily movement. Such warmups further indulge your body in different postures and motions in a low-stakes environment.

This warmup workout includes

- *Lunges*

- *Leg Circles*

- *Ankle Roll*

- *Shoulder roll*

- *Arm circles*

They must be done at least 10 to 15 times each.

1. **Static Stretching and Movement**

In this warmup exercise, you have to hold a position for an extended period. This helps to increase the flexibility of your body. It includes warmups like

- *Toe Touch*

- *Shoulder Stretch*

- *Chest Stretch*

- *Quad Stretches*

Types/Steps for Cooldown

No matter what level of exercise you do, a cooldown is as essential as a warmup because it helps to recover your body and prepare it for future performance. The cooldown is categorized into ***immediate, intermediate, and late phases***.

1. Immediate phase

This cooldown occurs when you come right after a run or when your heart rate is elevated, and your muscles are sore. After running, you can cool down by

- *Lowering your pace, like running slowly for 1 to 2 minutes*

- *Stop or suddenly stand*

- *Begin brisk walking*

In this way, you can lower your speed; otherwise, when you are running at your full pace and suddenly stop, your muscles of the extremities stop pumping blood to the heart and pool it instead. This situation limits blood circulation to the brain, and you may pass out.

1. Intermediate Phase

The intermediate cooldown phase occurs after it has decreased a little and your muscles are no longer fatigued. This kind is more suitable after a dynamic drill that helps the musculoskeletal system and strengthens flexibility. The intermediate cooldown involves

- *Quick jumps*

- *High knee skips*

- *Simple lunges*

- *Side-to-side shuffles*

All of these exercises can be done in two to three sets for not more than 15 to 30 seconds and helps to enhance your overall performance.

1. **Late phase**

The final kind of warming is done when the heart rate is back to normal; however, remember that how long you have to do this cool-down depends on the intensity of the exercise that you have done. Sometimes, this can take a while, even up to 2 to 4 hours. This involves exercises like

- *Full body stretches for a minimum of 5 to a maximum of 15 minutes*

Importance of Warm-up and Cool-down Exercises for Pickleball

Like other sports, before indulging in any other physical activity, your body needs to be prepared for any action to lose muscles. The best and most effective way to do so is simply to make a proper routine for your body by *adding warmups and workouts,* which help to reduce the stress on your heart and other muscles.

Why are warm-ups essential before pickleball?

Warmups may sound trivial, but in reality, they are not. This, with slower motion and pace, minimizes the intensity of any physical activity—helps to rev your cardiovascular

system while increasing the blood flow and body temperature. These warmups also reduce the risk of bodily injuries
and muscle soreness.

Why is cooldown important after warm-up?

On the other hand, the *cool-downs* relax your muscles from the warmups with gradual recovery before the
pre-exercise heart rate and blood pressure. Cooling down
the body is more important to regulate blood flow, especially in competitive endurance.

Let's take it by comparing jogging to driving on a mo-
torway. Similar to entering the on-ramp, the warm-up is
the acceleration phase. It gets your body ready for physical
exercise. The cooldown is the deceleration phase, similar to getting off the exit ramp when the body adjusts to
low-pace, regular activity.

*The cardiovascular system is also balanced by
cooling down*: Running causes your heart rate and car-
diac output to rise to move more oxygen-rich blood to
your working muscles and remove waste products from
them. Your extremity's muscles are supplied by blood ves-
sels, which enlarge to provide more effective blood flow
and speed up recuperation.

How do you warm up?

When you begin your workout session, start with the
warmup. Usually, the best way to proceed with the warmup
is by focusing on the large group of muscles like the ham-

string, followed by your pickleball-specific or other sports workouts.

To begin with, the warm-up starts with basic movements and activities of any exercise, then with a gradual motion, increase the intensity and speed (dynamic warm-up).

How do you cool down?

When you feel like your heart is racing, slowing down your pace is a cooldown in which you are still doing your physical activity but with a downward movement.

Which type of warmup is more beneficial for playing pickleball?

When it comes to warmups, especially for the pickleball game or any other paddle and racquet game, **dynamic warmups** are the best to boost bodily movement. This is because this kind of warmup involves your full body to warm up the muscles, stretches, and joints and enhances your flexibility.

Remember that you must maintain a balance, i .e. when you are doing the dynamic warm-up, the cooldown must be static with slow motion.

Benefits of Warm up before playing pickleball

Warming up before playing pickleball is essential to prepare your body to meet the physical demands of the pickleball game. Here are some of the benefits of warming up before playing pickleball

1. **Injury prevention**

Warming up helps to increase blood flow to your muscles and improve your joint mobility, and most importantly, it reduces the risk of injury. With the gradual increase in your heart rate and body temperature, you can prepare your body for the movements (up, down, back, and forth) to hit the shot.

1. **Improved performance**

Warming up can also help improve your performance on the court by adding more strength to your muscles and training them for every movement efficiently and promptly. You can move, react faster, and hit the ball more accurately by preparing your muscles and joints.

1. **Mental preparation**

Regular exercise reduces anxiety, so warming up can help you get into the right mindset for playing pickleball. It gives you time to focus your mind and mentally prepare for the game, which can help you perform better.

1. **Cardiovascular benefits**

Pickleball is a fast-paced sport requiring a prompt response to every shot. Warming up can help improve your cardiovascular endurance. By gradually increasing your heart rate, you can improve your stamina and reduce fatigue during the game.

The benefits are not restricted to it. There are many other advantages as well that are even more convenient.

Chapter Two

How to Use the Pickleball Routine

Warm-Up; How to use the pickleball routine?

P ickleball mainly involves six body parts: wrists, shoulders, ankles, hips, lower back, and knees. If these body parts are primed up properly, then it will be easy for you to hit every shot with ease. Slipping these makes you more likely to get hurt and injured.

Before getting into a pickleball game, the best practice is to *arrive before time; an hour or two, and do quick and easy warmups* for gentle and constant motion that primes your muscles. However, to prepare your body for the pickleball match, train your body with relevant workouts, along with dynamic warmup drills to your exercise routine.

Note: If you have any medical condition, consult your physician and get assistance from a licensed trainer.

As said, adding 5 to 10 minutes of warmups are essential for the pickleball game for training your muscles. This allows your body to stretch, while the cooldown will help bring your body back to normal and resting mode.

Here are some dynamic body warmups, cardiovascular exercises, to be precise, moves that will help your flexibility on the court.

Warmups and Cooldowns for Pickleball

Disclaimer: *Only perform those warmups that are physically easy for you. Otherwise, they can cause you severe injury. If you feel any pain or discomfort while doing any warmup exercise, it is suggested to stop immediately.*

Note: All of these exercises do not require any equipment. While doing these warmups and cool-down drills, maintain a proper breathing pattern and stay hydrated.

Let's get started.

1. **Core Twist**

This warmup drill is a great way to activate and engage your core muscles before playing pickleball. It helps to stabilize the spine and boosts your rotational power for rapid body movements like turning and twisting.

Target muscles

Core twist primarily targets your core muscles, including rectus abdominis, lower back muscles, and obliques.

How to do it?

Step 1: Lie down on your yoga mat while your legs are joined and arms are extended over your head.

Core twist warm-up

Step 2: Lift your legs in the air and arms off the ground. Squeeze your glute by engaging all your core muscles.

Step 3: Sit upwards and twist your body left and right without a break in a steady motion.

Core twist warm-up

Step 4: Return to your starting position and repeat 8 reps each for 3 sets.

Breathing Pattern

Inhale deeply through the nose in a neutral position, then exhale slowly through the mouth while twisting the torso. The exhale should be timed with the movement, and the breath should be fully expelled by the end of the twist.

Modification

You can also modify this exercise by adding a dumbbell or other weights to increase resistance and difficulty.

***

1. Knee Lifts/High Knees

This drill prepares your body for intense pickleball games and workouts. It will also boost your coordination, foot grip, body balance, and overall body muscles.

Target Muscles

Knee lifts and high knees involve your muscles, including the quadriceps, hamstrings, glutes, and hip flexors.

How to do it

Step 1: Place a box on the ground before you and stand with your spine straight.

Step 2: Step with your left foot on the box and lift your right knee in the air.

Knee lift posture 1

Step 3: Step your right foot down, switch your legs and repeat this warmup drill till you complete your sets.

Knee lift posture 2
Breathing Pattern

While doing this exercise, keep your chest wide open along with your shoulders and back, engaging your core. Breathe with a slow pattern while the movement is fast and continuous.

Modification

In case you do not have a box, you can use a medium-height stair.

***

1. Jumping Jacks

Jumping jacks are one of the most common warmups that increase your heart rate while adequately warming up your body muscles with blood circulation.

Target Muscles

This warmup primarily targets the glutes, quads, hip flexors, legs, abs, and shoulders as muscles.

How to do it?

While doing this warmup, you must maintain your proper posture and watch out for your breathing patterns. Keep your knees a little bent to land softly on the ground. Make sure your arms are extended and elbows are loose for a steady and smooth.

Step 1: Stand straight with your feet together and hands by your sides.

Jumping Jacks Posture 2

Step 2. Now jump and spread both feet and hands above your head.

Jumping Jacks Posture 2

Get back to position 1 and repeat this warm-up for 5 minutes.

Breathing Pattern

It depends on your fitness level. The best and most common technique is to inhale deeply from the nose and slowly exhale through your mouth when spreading your arms and legs apart.

Modification

To modify the jumping jack, you can perform it with *low impact or adjust the speed variation*. You can also *make it challenging* depending on your strength by adding a *resistance band*.

***

1. March in Place

This is a great exercise to get your heart rate without putting much strain on your joints; it is more like a low-impact cardio to warm up your muscles before you play pickleball.

Target muscles

This warmup will target your Hips and thighs mainly. Whereas legs, arms, core, and glute will also be involved.

How to do it?

Step 1: Bend your elbows at 90 degrees and stand straight with your feet apart (hip wide).

March in Place Posture 1

Step 2: Move your right elbow forward and raise your left knee.

March in Place Posture 2

Step 3: This exercise is more like walking while standing still. Repeat the exercise by switching your sides to complete your sets.

Breathing Pattern

Inhale through the nose for 2-3 steps and exhale through the mouth for 2-3 steps. Continue breathing in this pattern throughout the exercise.

Modification

You can increase the pace with your comfort and do arm circles or any other arm movement to engage your entire body.

***

1. Overhead Stretch

The overhead stretch can also be a standalone exercise as a part of your warmup routine. This helps to relieve your shoulder, upper back, and neck tension to improve your body posture.

Target muscles

Mainly, this warmup targets the upper body, including the shoulders, upper back, chest, and arms.

How to do it?

Step 1: Stand tall and straight with your feet and shoulder wide apart while your hands are on the sides.

Step 2: Raise your arms above your head while your elbows are straight

Overhead Stretch Posture 1

Step 3: Lock your fingers and turn your palms towards the ceiling or the sky.

Overhead Stretch Posture 2

Step 4: Hold in the same stretch for 10 to 30 seconds.

Step 5: Exhale and release your arms, lowering them back down to your sides.

Breathing Pattern

When raising your hand, inhale deeply when you raise your hands, hold it there for a while and then exhale slowly when you lower your arms.

Modification

You can march with high knees or strengthen your legs and use ankle weight to make it a bit more challenging.

***

1. Crab Toe Touches

The crab toe touches are a dynamic cardio workout warmup that helps to improve your agility. This also strengthens your core and boosts your metabolism.

Target Muscles

The primary target muscles for this exercise are the lower back and abs. At the same time, it targets your hamstring, glutes, and shoulders as your secondary muscles.

How to do it

Step 1: Take your yoga mat and sit on it while bending your knee. Place your hands behind you while your feet are joined together.

Step 2: Lift your hips off the mat, kick in the air with your right leg and touch your toes with your left hand.

Crab toe touch Posture 1

Step 3: Repeat the procedure with your left leg, touch your toes with your right hand, and keep alternating until your reps are completed.

Crab toe touch Posture 2
Breathing Pattern

You have to maintain a regular and steady breathing pattern.

Modification

You can make it easy by simply skipping the hip lift and raising your legs only.

***

1. Hamstring Kicks

The hamstring kick exercise is a great way to warm your leg muscles and increase your body flexibility. It can also help to improve your coordination and balance, along with engaging your core muscle.

Target muscles

The hamstring kicks exercise primarily targets the muscles on the back of your thighs. These muscles include the biceps femoris, semimembranosus, and semitendinosus. Also, your glutes and quadriceps but only a little.**How to do it?**

Step 1: Stand tall with a straight spine, your feet hip-width apart, and your arms at your sides.

Step 2: Lift your right knee towards your chest while keeping your left leg down to the ground.

Hamstring Kick Posture 1

Step 3: Extend your right leg, keeping it straight and flexing your foot to engage your hamstring muscles.

Hamstring Kick Posture 2

Step 4: Bring your right leg back to the ground, lift your left knee towards your chest, and repeat the movement on the other side.

Step 5: Continue alternating between your left and right legs, kicking your legs up towards your buttocks and feeling the stretch in your hamstrings.

Breathing Pattern

inhale deeply as you lift one leg and exhale forcefully as you kick that leg forward, engaging your core muscles. Then, inhale as you lower the leg back down and exhale as you repeat the same movement with the other leg.

Modification

To increase the intensity of the exercise, you can add arm movements by swinging your arms in opposition to your legs in an upward direction or side.

1. Arm Swing

This warmup drill effectively prepares your upper body by increasing your heart rate and allowing your body to be ready for an intense pickleball game.

Target muscles

It targets your upper body muscles, including the shoulders, chest, and your upper back. When your arms are swinging, it will engage your core muscles, but you have to keep your movements controlled.

How to do it?

Step 1: Start this warmup by standing with your feet hip-width apart, and your arms must be at your sides.

Arm Swing Posture 1

Step 2: Swing your right arm forward direction at your front and bring them back as far as possible.

Arm Swing Posture 2

Step 3: Repeat the steps again with your other arm in both directions. Continue swinging your arms back and forth in a fluid motion, alternating between your left and right arms.

Breathing Pattern

During arm swing exercise, the breathing pattern should be rhythmic and natural. Inhale through your nose as you bring your arms forward, and exhale through your mouth as you swing them back. Keep the breaths steady and consistent with the movement of your arms.

Modification

To increase the intensity of the exercise, you can add a slight hop or jump as you swing your arms. You can also add weights, holding them in both hands.

***

1. Jogging

Jogging is the most common and great way to improve your cardiovascular fitness and endurance, not only for burning calories but also for strengthening your leg muscles. It may seem easy, but it could be tiresome, and you must do it correctly.

Target muscles

Jogging targets the quadriceps, hamstring, glutes, core muscles, and calves.

How to do it?

Step 1: Strand straight with your feet hip-width apart and your arms placed at your sides.

Jogging Posture 1

Step 2: Start to move your feet in a running motion, lifting your knees upwards near your chest and alternating your legs as you go. When you are jogging, keep your upper body and shoulder relaxed and down to the back.

Jogging Posture 2

Step 3: Swing your arms back and forth, and try to keep your elbows at a 90-degree angle straight. While running, engage your core and pull back your stomach towards your spine.

Try to maintain a steady pace; you can do it in your court by reaching before time.

Breathing Pattern

A good breathing pattern for jogging is to inhale through your nose for two or three strides and then exhale through your mouth for two or three strides.

Modification

This warm-up can also be done for strength building while standing still at the same place and running motion. Increase your speed gradually as you become more comfortable with the movement.

***

1. Butt Kickers

This exercise is perfect for increasing knee and hip flexibility by engaging your core muscles.

Target muscles

The primary target of this warm-up is the quadriceps and glutes.

How to do it?

Step 1: Stand straight with your feet hip-width apart and your arms hanging at your sides.

Step 2: Start jogging by standing in a place, lifting your heels toward your buttocks with each step.

Butt Kicks 1

Step 3: Aim to touch your heels to your glutes with each step, your knees close together and your core engaged.

Butt kicks 2
Breathing Pattern

Inhale deeply through the nose during the initial step of bringing your heel up towards your glutes, and then exhale fully through the mouth as you release your foot back down to the ground.
Modification

To improve your warmup, you can increase or decrease your body movement.

***

Chapter Three

Warm-up and Cool Down

Easy Warmup Drills for Seniors

Some body parts like the shoulder, neck, knees, hips, and lower back get stiff with age and can also be problematic for seniors more often. Your injury chances increase if they become in motion intensely and too soon.

Although it seems tempting to jump like a teenager, with age, it will become tough for the older players to do vigorous warmups like every other pickleball player, as it adds more stress to the heart, which is challenging for the elders. Hence, to build up their stamina, we have lined up some easy yet efficient warmups and cooldowns for older ones. This includes

1. Side-by-side squats

This warmup exercise commonly strengthens the lower body muscles to hit every low-level shot. While doing this exercise, you must keep your abs and glutes tight with your head up and glute tight.

Target muscles

It mainly focuses on the quads, glutes, hamstring, and core of your body.

How to do it?

Step 1: Stand in a position where your feet are apart shoulder wide.

Side-by-side squats posture 1

Step 2: Put pressure on your hips and pose like sitting in the air. Hold in the same posture for a few seconds, stand up, take a side step, and return to your original position.

Side-by-side squats Posture 2

Step 3: Repeat the same exercise by shifting the sides.

Side Squats postures

Breathing Pattern

Inhale when you lower your body and exhale when you push off your bent leg.

Modification

If you cannot do these squats, you can modify them by doing wall squats.

***

1. **Walking lunges**

The walking lunges tone the sculpt and strengthen your glutes and leg by improving the flexibility of your hips. This increases the flexibility and stability of your body by engaging your core.

Target muscles

The walking lunges target the glutes, hamstring, and quads.

How to do it?

Step 1: Stand straight on your feet with hip-width apart, step forward, and gradually bend your knees till your back knee is above the floor.

Walking Lunges Posture 1

Step 2: Stand back up, step forward with your left foot, and bend both knees precisely as you did before.

Walking Lunges Posture 2

Step 3: Repeat the process and stay in the posture for 30 seconds at least.

Breathing Pattern

Inhale deeply before starting your lunges drill and exhale when you lunge forward.

Modification

If you are not comfortable with the chair, you can also do this with exercise by taking support from a wall.

***

1. Arm Circles

Arm circles are the basic and most popular warmup you might have done back in high school as well. This helps incorporate the beginning of any workout for your upper body to prevent muscle injury, prepare you for strength training, and engage your core muscle.

Target Muscles

This warm-up targets the shoulders as primary muscles and the upper back as secondary muscles.

How to do it?

Step 1: Stand straight by parting your feet at your shoulder width.

Step 2: Open your arms widely and raise them in the air on the sides without bending your elbows.

Step 3: Gradually rotate your arms forward and make small circles, more likely in a diameter of approximately 1 foot.

Arm Circles Posture

Step 4: Complete a set by making circles clockwise and then switch your hands counterclockwise.

Breathing Pattern

The breathing pattern for this drill varies depending on your personal preference. However, it is recommended to inhale deeply when you are lifting your arms.

Modification

You can start with small circles, and then gradually, you can make bigger circles with slow to moderate motion.

***

1. Shoulder Squeeze

One of the easiest warmups seniors can perform should squeeze, which can be done before your workout routine and in the court before going into the pickleball court.

Target Muscles

Shoulder stretch targets the muscles of your upper body
How to do it?
Step 1: Stand tall with a straight back and apart your feet with hip-width.
Step 2: Pull back your elbows while your hands open and squeeze your shoulder blades.

Shoulder squeeze posture 1
Step 3: Hold this posture and keep squeezing your shoulders

Shoulder squeeze posture 2
Breathing Pattern

Inhale deeply with your nose and exhale from your mouth when releasing the tension from your shoulders.

Modifications

You can take the support of the wall for that warmup. Besides that, you can add a *shoulder squeeze reverse lunge* with the same warm-up exercise. For that, you will need to

Step 1: Stand by parting your feet hip-width and raise your arms until they parallel the floor.

Posture 1

Step 2: Step backward with your left foot and flex your knees till the back knee is just above the floor.

Step 3: Bend your elbows on your back until the shoulder blades are together.

Posture 2
Step 4: Stand up back, straighten your arms, and repeat the procedure with your right leg.

Posture 3
Complete your rep while switching your legs.

Posture 4

Note: The modification exercise is not compulsory; you can do it only if you are comfortable.

***

1. Torso Rotation

This warmup exercise enhances flexibility, posture, and strength from the core to endurance. Although it is simple, it helps to be more active each day.

Target Muscles

It targets your core, spine, legs and arm muscles mainly.

How to do it?

Step 1: Stand with your feet hip-width apart while your knees must be bent slightly.

Posture 1: Torso Rotation

Step 2: Stretch your arms in front of you and clasp them together.

Step 3: Rotate your torso slowly from one side to another, keep your shoulder down, and engage your core. Make sure your waist is turning while your arms stay static.

Torso Rotation Posture 2

Breathing Pattern

When doing the twist, inhale slowly and deeply and exhale similarly when turning back to your original position.

Modification

You can do this warmup exercise by sitting on a chair like this.

Torso Rotation posture 3

Note: This warmup is not recommended for people with osteoporosis.

***

1. Wrist rotation/circles

This warmup is an essential drill for your arm and wrist movement as it will help to support your hand movement when hitting the pickleball.

Target Muscles

This warmup drill will target your forearm, wrist, flexor and extensor muscles.

How to do it

Step 1: Stand or sit (whatever your posture is comfortable) while your back should be straight and your arms extended in front of you, with your face forward.

Step 2: Clasp your hand together by locking your fingers loosely.

Wrist Circles Posture 1

Step 3: Slowly start rotating your hands and rotating your wrists in a circular motion. Move them as far as you can comfortably do.

Wrist Circles Posture 2

Step 4: Repeat the circular motion for 10-15 rotations and then reverse the direction of the rotation, starting with your palms facing up and moving them down, then up again.

Breathing Pattern

While performing this drill, you need to inhale deeply and slowly. Bring your wrist towards your body and exhale slowly as you perform this exercise.

Modification

It is an easy and straightforward workout; you can reduce the range of motion if starting for the first time and increase the intensity later. Also, you can add resistance by adding lighter grips.

***

1. **Ankle Circles**

Ankle circles are essential for seniors to prepare for a pickleball game.

Target Muscles

This drill will involve your ankles primarily, while the feet and calves will be targeted as your secondary muscles.

How to do it

Step 1: Stand straight with your feet hip wide and arms at your sides.

Ankle Circle Posture 1

Step 2: Lift one foot off the ground and extend your leg before you.

Step 3: Rotate your ankle in a circular motion, making sure to move through the full range of motion.

Ankle Circles Posture 2

Step 4: Repeat the ankle circles in the opposite direction. Switch to the other foot and repeat the same steps.

Ankle Circle Posture 3
Breathing Pattern

Breathe slowly and lightly while performing this drill. Begin your drill with small circles and then, with a gradual motion, increase the diameter to open your ankle joints as much as you can.

Modification

You can perform this exercise by sitting on a bench or a chair.

***

1. Standing/Seated Spiral Twist

The stretch for this exercise is *a standing or seated spiral twist* that helps to strengthen your spine and enhances your flexibility and spinal mobility.

Target muscles

This exercise targets your spine, lower back, and hips and engages oblique muscles.

How to do it?

Step 1: Stand with your feet hip-width apart and your arms by your sides.

Standing Spiral twist Posture 1

Step 2: Open your hands to their actual length, ensure the elbows are straight, and cross your legs.

Standing Spiral twist Posture 2

Step 3: Twist on your right side and hold the twist for a few seconds while maintaining balance.

Step 4: Inhale deeply again, and as you exhale, release the twist and return to the starting position.

Step 5: Repeat the twist on the other side, placing your right hand on your left hip and your left hand behind your back.

Step 6: Hold the twist for a few seconds before releasing and returning to the starting position. Continue alternating twists for several repetitions, maintaining good posture and balance throughout the exercise.

Breathing Pattern

Inhale deeply through your nose and exhale from your mouth by engaging your core muscles.

***

1. Calf Raise

Calf raise is a great workout drill that targets your lower legs and back muscles to support your spine, allowing more stability.

Target Muscles

The primary muscles involved in this drill are the claves, gastrocnemius muscles and your lower leg.

How to do it

Step 1: Stand with a straight torso while your feet will be hip wide apart and your toes are pointing in the forward direction.

Calves Squeeze 1

Step 2: Slowly raise your heels off the ground and try to squeeze your calves as you can comfortably do.

Calves Squeeze 2

Step 3: Slowly return back to your starting position by lowering your heels and repeating the set.

Modification

You can modify this drill by changing your tempo and adding resistance; for instance, you can hold weights in your both hands.

Breathing Pattern

When lowering your heels, breathe in and slowly return to your original position.

***

1. Side Steps

One commonly used pickleball movement is the side-step or the side shuffles. The side steps warm-up is a simple and effective way to warm up your lower body muscles and increase your heart rate before the big game. It can help to improve your balance, coordination, and agility, preparing you for the movement. Hence, strengthening and warming up your leg muscles are side steps.

Target muscles

This warmup will target your glutes, things, quadriceps, and hamstrings to meet pickleball's back-and-forth movement.

How to do it?

Step 1: Stand with your feet and shoulders wide apart with your arms on your sides.

Side Step Posture 1

Step 2: Step to the right with your right foot, keeping your left foot planted.

Side Step Posture 2

Step 3: Bring your left foot towards your right foot and close your feet together.

Step 4: Step to the left with your left foot, keeping your right foot static as you have done before.

Step 5: Bring your right foot towards your left foot, closing your feet together. Continue stepping side to side, keeping your core engaged and your movements controlled.

Breathing Pattern

It depends on your personal preference and your side step intensity of your side kicks. However, the recommended pattern is to inhale deeply from the nose and exhale gradually from your mouth.

Modification

To increase the intensity of the warm-up, try adding arm movements. For example, you can swing your arms side to side as you step or raise them above your head and lower them to your sides as you step.

***

Chapter Four

Cooldown after Warmup for Pickleball for all Players

Whether you are up for an intense pickleball game or a body workout for strength-building training, you need to cool down to restore your heart rate to its original position. For instance, after doing squats, you can perform a light aerobic activity like walking on the treadmill for a minimum of five minutes to cool down.

Some easiest cool down are

1. **Wrist Stretch**

This one is most important for pickleball players as it involves stretching wrists, hands, and fingers to cool down. To perform this,

Step 1: Stand up straight and extend your right arm in the forward direction at shoulder height.

Step 2: Grasp your right hand with your left hand by keeping your elbows straight.

Wrist Stretch Posture 1

Step 3: Bend your wrist in a backward direction till you feel a stretch in your forearm.

Wrist Stretch Posture 2

Step 4: Next, bend your wrist in a downward direction.
Step 5: Repeat this and keep switching your arms.

***

1. Standing quad stretch

For the cool down, the ***standing quad stretch*** is recommended for elders. To do it,

Step 1: Take the support of a chair; stand on your feet while your hand rests on the back of the chair.

Step 2: Bend your left knee and take back your leg. With the help of your left hand, pull it towards your hips.

Step 3: Stretch as much as possible for 30 seconds in the same position.

Standing quad stretch
This exercise is itself a cool-down for exercise that targets the muscles of your upper body.

***

1. Quadriceps Stretchs

Step 1: Bend your right knee and bring your right heel in
an upward direction toward your hips.
Step 2: Hold the right ankle with your hands, stay in the
same posture for 30 seconds, and repeat with the other leg
2 to 3 times.

Quadriceps Stretches

***

1. Laydown Core Stretch

The core stretch puts a lot of stress on your spine. Hence, slowly returning to your original position and holding there for 5 to 10 seconds before doing your excellent down is essential.

To cool down,

Step 1: lay down straight in the resting position while hands on your ground, take deep breaths, and take them out.

Cooldown Core twist Posture

***

1. Hamstring stretch

Step 1: Stand straight and cross your legs by placing your right leg in front of your left leg.

Step 2: Bend slowly by lowering your forehead to your right knee and keep your knees straight.

Hamstring Cooldown posture

Step 3: Hold on in this posture for 15 to 20 seconds and then repeat it by placing your left leg in front and right in the back.

***

1. Calf muscle cooldown

Step 1: Stand by holding on to the arms with the support of a wall while your toes point forward.

Step 2: By keeping your right foot flat on the floor, extend your same leg backward.

Step 3: Slightly bend your knee, lean forward, and bend your left knee until you feel a stretch in your back calf.

Calf Stretch

Step 4: Hold in there for a while and repeat on the left leg.

1. Glute Stretch

Step 1: Lie down on the ground with a straight back and bend your knees.

Step 2: Cross your right leg on your left and bring both knees towards your chest.

Step 3: Pull the left leg towards you till you feel a stretch in your glutes.

Glute Stretch

Step 4: Hold in the same position for at least 30 seconds.

***

1. Lower Back Stretch

To perform that

Step 1: Lie down on your back and bring both knees to your chest

Step 2: With a gradual motion, pull back your knees towards your shoulders till you feel the stretch on your lower back.

Lower Back Stretch
Step 3: Hold back in the position for 10 to 20 seconds.

***

1. Shoulder Stretch

For this,
Step 1: Bring your arms across your upper body and hold them straight.

Shoulder Stretch 1
Step 2: With your other arm, grasp your elbow and pull them towards your chest.

Shoulder Stretch 2

Step 3: Hold for at least 10 to 20 seconds and repeat on the other side.

***

1. **Hip Flexor Stretch**

When performing this, keep your body in a neutral position while your face is in the forward direction. To perform this,

Step 1: Knee down your right leg and bend the other in the front at 90 degrees.

Step 2: Move your weight forward until you feel a hip stretch.

Hip Flexor Stretch

Step 3: Repeat this stretch to cool down and keep shifting your legs.

***

Chapter Five

What Exercises Build Strength for Pickleball Players?

W hether a new or an expert player, the aim is to win the game no matter what your opponent's playing level; we want to be the best in every way and win the game. This can be possible only if you have the stronger muscles to exert the required effort with strength in your game.

Most of the time, the answer to gaining strength is to lift weights; it sounds simple and easy, but they are tough. Also, this is not feasible for every player, especially of older age, so we have to look for some alternatives such as strengthening training.

As of now, you know that your pickleball player needs more strength because of the more body movement in the game; strengthening workouts helps to achieve more power, especially when you are playing. The best strength training exercises for pickleball players that are recommended by professionals are

- *Split squats:* contribute to muscles to allow to run faster

- *Single leg deadlift:* helps to maintain balance and strengthens hip muscles

- *Dumbbell chest press:* strengthens shoulders and builds chest, allowing better swing

- *Goblet Squats:* boosts your leg strength

- *Dumbbell Lawnmower Rows:* focuses on building your back muscles and obliques

Why is strength training an essential workout for pickleball players?

Pickleball players must be more active and have less or no body fat or extra weight room, which is necessary to improve their game. However, when it comes to the significance of strengthening training, here are the top three reasons why you need them.

1. Boost power and performance overall

When playing pickleball, you will need more power to become better or best at your game; hence, for that, you need to build your muscles to boost your strength. For instance, you will need more force to hit a fastball. Adding strength training to your routine will improve your hand swing, and you can hit the ball harder.

1. Your speed will be improved

If you have strong muscles, then obviously, the running will be fast, which means you will have more endurance to chase and return every shot. This cannot be achieved with weight lifting only. However, if you are strong and have been working on your boosted stamina exercises, hitting the ball becomes easier, and you can do it for a long time.

1. The risk of injury is minimized

Weight lifting exercise specifically decreases the risk of injuries if you already deal with previous injuries. This targets your muscles and bones altogether, along with tendons, ligaments, and other joints, automatically minimizing the risk of injuries.

Remember that, when working on your strength training, do not focus on the wrist only, as it alone will not be enough for a pickleball game.

That is why you need to keep all the moments like simulated hitting, rotating, running, lunging, and squatting together. Thus, this strengthening training will cover them all.

The Five Best Strength training exercises are

These are five simple strength training exercises that you can easily add to your existing workout routine that you have or repeat twice a week on alternative days to target all the muscles. The five strength training exercises are

1. Split squats

As the pickleball shots are not predictable, and you have to drop down on your knees or on your hips, in short, it requires bending. The split squats help to build your leg strength. Here is how you perform this workout.

Targeted Muscles

This exercise will target your quadriceps, glutes, and your hamstrings in this exercise, along with lower back and abdominal muscles.

How to do it?

Step 1: Hold dumbbells in both hands in a standing position.

Step 2: One step forward with your right foot so that both your feet are apart

Step 3: Lift your back heel in the air, or you can take the support of a bench.

Step 4: Bend both knees to lower yourself and go as low as possible without touching the ground.

Step 5: Complete the reps and then switch to your other leg.

Alternative method

This training can be done in an easier way; you can remove the weights (dumbbells) from this exercise and hold on to a chair or any railing.

Cooldown

When you feel your heart racing, start with a light aerobic activity while walking for five minutes, and then foam rolls your outer and inner thighs, calves, and mid-back.

1. Single-leg deadlift

This exercise is to boost your body balance and coordination for leg muscles.

Targeted Muscles

The primary targeted muscle for this training is the hamstring, along with the glute maximus and gluteus medius, while the lower muscles will help to stand you up from the bottom movement.

How to do it?

Step 1: Take the weight and hold it in your left hand.

Step 2: Kick in the air with your left leg backward and lean forward with your torso

Step 3: Slightly bend your right knee and reach down as far as your other (left) hand

Step 4: Stand up back and put your left foot on the ground

Step 5: Repeat till you reach your desired reps. Do not forget to change your legs.

Modification

When working with the weights, shift them in each hand. To maintain balance, you can hold on to something steady with your other (free) hand, or to make it tough, hold another weight in the free hand.

Cooldown

When done with the training, switch to Toe to Toe wall stretch to cool down. For that, you need to stand at least 12 to 15 inches away, lift your right foot, and press it against the ball and toes while your heels are placed firmly on the ground. To deeper your stretch, take your toes as high as you can.

Toe-to-Toe Wall stretch

1. Dumbbell chest press

Pickleball works with a single hand (either right or left). Hence this exercise is important to boost the booth arm support, and each arm works independently, which helps to correct and balance the strength of both arms.

Targeted Muscles

This exercise focuses on the upper body, mainly the chest muscles, and supports the tricep muscles.

How to do it?

Step 1: Hold the dumbbells in both your hands and lay down on your back on the bench

Step 2: Hold and press the weights upwards toward the ceilings until your arms are in a straight posture.

Step 3: Turn your head in a direction so that your palms are facing your feet

Step 4: Lower the weights till they touch the outer side of your chest muscles

Step 5: Press the dumbbells back up till the elbows are straight

Dumbbell chest press

Modification

To make this exercise easy, start with your lower weights instead or start with a single hand first and then gradually shift to the other hand.

Cooldown

For that, the overhead triceps and shoulder stretch.

Step 1: Stand or sit tall with a straight spine, take your arms above your head, and drop your forearm on your back between your shoulder blades.

Step 2: Grab the area above your head with the bent elbow and pull it slowly until you feel a stretch in your shoulder and the back of your arm.

Overhead Tricep
1. Goblet Squats

The main purpose of squats exercise is only to strengthen your legs and lower body muscles along with allowing you to explosively jump out from one posture to the other. This one is perfect training for legs to hit the lower shots of pickleball.

Target Muscles

It targets the glutes, quadriceps, and a few hamstrings; your lower body will be used mostly, involving abdominals and lower back muscles to stabilize your torso. The weights will help to support your biceps and shoulder muscles.

How to do it?

Step 1: Hold your kettlebell in both hands in front of your chest

Step 2: Place your feet apart, slightly wider than your shoulder width

Step 3: Squat as low as you can do comfortably while your weight keeps in front of your chest

Step 4: Stand back up to complete and repeat your rep

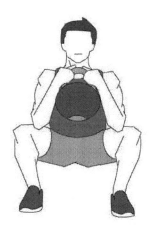

Goblet Squats

Modification

For weights, in case you do not have a kettlebell available, you can use dumbbells instead; if you want it harder, rest these weights on your shoulders.

Cool Down

For cool down, the best one is a standing Quadriceps stretch.

Step 1: Bend your right knee and bring your right heel in an upward direction toward your hips.

Step 2: Hold the right ankle with your hands, stay in the same posture for 30 seconds, and repeat with the other leg 2 to 3 times.

Quadriceps Stretches
1. Dumbbell Lawnmower Rows

This exercise is named as it is similar to starting a lawn-mower (if you are familiar with it only). This will help to strengthen your core to rotate, allowing you to support your forehand and backhand movement in a pickleball game.

Target muscles

As you lift, the quadriceps and hamstrings will stabilize your legs, while the , , and in your back will help in lifting your biceps and upper body.

How to do it?

Step 1: Mold your body in the lunges posture with a foot forward and backward

Step 2: Place the dumbbell next to your forwarded foot on the ground

Step 3: Place your forearm on the forwarded leg

Step 4: Grab the grounded dumbbell on your rare arm

Dumbbell Lawnmower Rows

Step 5: Pull it upward to the length of your stomach and slightly rotate it with your shoulder

Step 6: Put the weight back to the ground and repeat the reps, then switch your leg

Modification

To begin with it or make it easy, place your knee and your hand on the front for support on a bench. This way, your leg movement will be limited.

Cooldown

To cool down after doing dumbbell lawnmower rows, perform overhead triceps (check how to do overhead triceps under strengthening training no. 3).

***

How can you incorporate strength training into your pickleball routine?

When you are already doing your workout routine, you need to maintain a balanced plan instead of cramming all in a single day. The best method is to spread them over a week as much as possible, along with a rest day after strength training so that your muscles can recover.

As a new player, doing each exercise twice a week and a minimum of 45 minutes of workout or so is recommended.

Keep in mind that you have to focus on your form mainly, not on the intensity, the power you have, or the speed. Be vigilant that you are doing any exercise in the wrong way that results in muscle injury that will take a while to recover correctly.

Chapter Six

Preparing Yourself for Pickleball

How to prepare yourself physically and mentally for a pickleball tournament?

S o, if you are playing pickleball for the first time, you must be prepared physically and mentally to be in the game with all your heart and mind to give your 100%. Here are a few steps to help you prepare whether you are playing singles or doubles tournament.

How to get prepared for a Pickleball tournament physically?

When we speak of getting ready and preparing yourself for the pickleball game, it is more than just hitting the ball. You are more likely to get hurt and injured if you neglect the physical requirements before and after your game. What you need to do is

1. Stay hydrated properly

Keep your body hydrated by drinking enough water when your pickleball match is lined up and on the tournament. Staying hydrated will remain fresh and prevents dizziness and feeling of tiredness.

In a nutshell, it is necessary to drink an adequate amount of water, for instance, a player with *160 lbs. should take at least 80 oz.* of water per day (an ounce per pound of your body weight).

This way, your body will remain hydrated throughout; however, if you intake water on the day of your match, you will have frequent trips to the restroom, which will lose the temperament of the match.

1. Stay healthy by eating well

To stay energized, you need to get a quality diet with well-round meals, which plays a vital role in your muscle's strength and recovery. You need to start taking care of it before your tournament. All you need to focus on is to take a healthy and minimal diet a day before your competition.

1. Practice makes you work like a pro

Obviously, one of the keys to becoming a pro is to keep practicing. In case you are playing with doubles or singles, it is always recommended to prepare with your partner and work on your tactics and style. This helps to create a competitive environment for you, and also, you will be able to get the pressure.

In case you have no one to play with, no worries, you can get a pickleball shooter and practice your strategies.

***

How to prepare yourself for pickleball mentally?

Preparing yourself for a pickleball game mentally is as significant as it is physically; it must not be underestimated as it helps you to focus more on your game. It is important to get ready for any racquet game, whether it is pickleball, tennis, or any other game. Here is some advice to cope with pickleball tournament anxiety.

1. **Plan your game ahead**

Not only for a game but overall, it is important for every person to plan and be organized. Planning ahead helps to release at least half of your anxiety; make a list that a day before that what you will need in your game and/or what you will need when you are traveling.

1. **Be on time; arrive early before your game**

As a part of being organized, the next thing that you need to practice is to be on time instead of arriving exactly before your match. Reaching there before time will help you to perform warm-up on the court, which will also help you to get used-to to the pickleball court.

Not only this, arriving earlier will make you get familiar with the organizers and the tournament rules to avoid inconvenience.

1. Take deep breaths

Getting anxious before your big game or tournament is natural, so do not get panic about it; instead, take deep breaths and try to get more oxygen in your lungs. This trick helps to relax your body and mind and maintain a positive attitude.

1. Visualize in your mind that you are already winning the game

Imagining a positive image, such as that you are winning the game, helps to maintain a positive attitude and deletes negative thoughts.

This helps to boost your gaming spirit and gives you a push. Here what we suggest is to stay motivated with keeping in mind that you can win and stay confident but not over-confident, as it may lead you to disappointment.

1. Takes short breaks within matches

Take small breaks between the match (if possible) and relax to get recharged for the next spell. This trick will keep you focused; drink some water to hydrate yourself by drinking water.

1. Stay focused and don't compare yourself with others

The most important thing is to stay focused; everyone has their own method, style, and his own tricks of playing. If someone is doing something different, it does not mean you are doing it wrong. You have your own skillset that is incomparable with other players, so **be yourself.**

***

What diet should you take during/after pickleball warmups?

During or after the warmup of pickleball, along with staying hydrated, it is essential to take light meals or snacks that provide enough energy to fuel your body. However, you have to ensure it does not cause digestive issues.

Here is some bland food you can take before the pickleball warm-up. It includes

Fruits: In fruits, you can take fresh fruit, including bananas, apples, and grapes, that have natural sugar, which maintains your blood sugar as well as fiber and will keep you hydrated.

Nuts and seeds: You can have seeds and nuts like almonds, walnuts, or pumpkin seeds, as they are excellent sources of protein and healthy fats to sustain your energy level during your warm-up

Yogurt: Take Greek or low-fat yogurt is also a great source of protein and calcium that helps to rebuild your muscles.

Smoothies: Using fresh or frozen fruit, yogurt, or protein powder can be a quick and easy option to have all the nutrients and energy in your body.

Whole grain toast: you can also have whole grain toast with peanut butter, or avocado is an excellent source of carbohydrates and healthy fats that helps to retain your energy level.

So, feel free to add these food items to your diet before/during/after warmups, not only for pickleball but for everybody's exertion.

*****

Recommendations and Preventions for Pickleball Warm-Up Drill

Pickleball is equally suitable for indoor and outdoor sports played by people of every age and skill level. As it is a fast-paced game, this sport requires more physical activity. Hence, warm-up exercises are significant in every pickleball game to prevent muscular injuries.

Here are some related guidelines in case you encounter any injury.

How can I recover after pickleball?

Playing pickleball is itself a complete exercise as it adds more back-and-forth movement compared to other sports like tennis or ping pong. Hence, there are chances that you might get hurt or injured even after proper warmup and exercise. In that case, here is what you need to do.

1. **Follow the rule of R.I.C.E**

R.I.C.E is the short form of relax, ice, compress, and elevate. You need to rest the body, whichever body part hurts. If it is sore, use ice to minimize pain and swelling, compress it with the help of a bandage in case of swelling and elevate the hurt body part.

Hence, altogether, they help to recover the body with ease.

1. Get a better sleep

What is better than having a good and sound sleep—that is precisely the best way to recharge and recover yourself before and after a pickleball game. Make sure to have at least 8 to 10 hours of sleep to prep and relax your body.

1. Plan a relaxing bath

The next best option is to have a relaxing hot or ice bath as both help effectively to recover from physical activities. If you are tired from workout sessions, an ice-cold bath is what you need.

On the other hand, a hot bath helps to soothe a tired body because heat improves blood circulation, which results in releasing muscle tension with instant recovery.

1. Do stretches or YOGA

After a pickleball game, light cooldown helps the muscle to lose tension and improves flexibility for the long term. For that, you can either go for your regular stretches or Yoga because body stretching bring your body to its natural position.

1. Indulge yourself in full body workout

In case you are taking a break from pickleball, it is suggested to keep your body active and boost the strength of your muscles. Regular exercise prepares your body for your game without causing any fatigue on your body.

1. Watch out for your physical stamina

No matter how healthy and strong you are, there is a limit to your stamina. Whenever you feel like you have reached your maximum limit, you much take a break before you reach the point where you burn out.

1. Get yourself a massage

The best way to relax your body is by getting a massage to ease muscle tightness and tension, which helps improve blood circulation. This, to some extent, will also help to relax your mind.

1. Healthy diet

Finally, with all these tricks, the final step is to have a healthy diet and regular exercise. Ensure you are taking enough protein, carbs, and vegetables at a balanced level.

How can I prevent leg cramps during/after a pickleball game?

The clutching pain in the legs is more likely to affect older players than young adults. This involuntary *sharp pain pops up in the calf, foot, or thigh muscles*, causing nerve issues and fatigue, limiting your movement and endless hours.

As said, *older players are more prone to leg cramps* because *the tendons shorten with time*, causing these cramps during an intense game. Other common and possible reasons are *dehydration, heavy exercise without a warmup, and stress*.

How to prevent leg cramps?

Here are some trusted preventions for leg cramps.

- *Keep yourself hydrated. Try to drink a minimum of 100 oz. Water per day. It will make you go to the restroom frequently but will reduce the leg cramps*

- *Exercise and play pickleball regularly*

- *Stretch your calves and legs before and after the activity. This will help to minimize the stress and tension in the legs*

- *Take proper vitamins. Vitamin B12 is best and recommended by medical representatives who effectively reduce leg cramps*

How to treat leg cramps?

The best and most effective method to stop leg clamps is stretching the muscle, clenching, or flexing your foot, leg, or toes. You can also rub your affected muscle to release it and reduce the tension.

Conclusion

C onclusively, warmups and cooldowns are essential to every game, especially for pickleball, because it requires more back-and-forth movements. Taking the proper time and making warm-ups a part of your routine with proper cool-downs possess many benefits, such as strengthening the muscles and preparing them for an intense game.

The aim of this guide is to help pickleball players of all ages and skill levels with appropriate warmup stretching and cooldowns that ideally mimic the game's movements. This way, you will care for your body by preventing severe injuries.

Other Books By Author

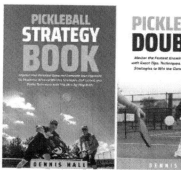

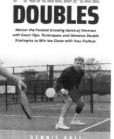

*CLICK HERE TO SEE OTH-
ER AUTHORS' BOOKS ON AMA-
ZON!*

Thank You

Thank you for buying my book and I hope you enjoyed it. If you found any value in this book I would really appreciate it if you'd take a minute to post a review about this book. I check all my reviews and love to get feedback.

This is the real reward for me knowing that I'm helping others. If you know anyone who may enjoy this book, please share the message and gift it to them.

References

1. *The 5 best warmups to Boost Your Pickleball Performance (no date) Paddletek Pickleball. Available at: https://www.paddletek.com/blogs/news/5-pickleb all-warmups#:~:text=Dynamic%20stretches%20 are%20perhaps%20the,your%20performance%2 0and%20prevent%20injuries. (Accessed: May 2, 2023).*

2. *6 best exercises to do right before you play pickleball (2023) SilverSneakers. Available at: https://www.silversneakers.com/blog/6-best-e xercises-do-before-pickleball/ (Accessed: May 2, 2023).*

3. *Amy Marturana Winderl, C.P.T. (2018) 10 great stretches to do after a lower-body workout, SELF. SELF. Available at: https://www.self.com/galle ry/great-lower-body-stretches (Accessed: May 2, 2023).*

4. *Azevedo, J. (no date) The 7 best warm-ups for tennis and pickleball, the. Available*

at: *https://www.thepaseoclub.com/blog/seven-bes t-warm-ups-tennis-pickleball (Accessed: May 2, 2023).*

5. Pickleball University (2022) *Advice for pickleball tournament anxiety, Pickleball University. Pickleball University. Available at: https://www.pickleballuniversity.com/home/advic e-for-pickleball-tournament-anxiety#:~:text=Bre athe,play%20pickleball%20to%20begin%20with . (Accessed: May 2, 2023).*

6. Pickleball University (2022) *Pickleball University blog: Pickleball warm ups and cool downs, Pickleball University. Pickleball University. Available at: https://www.pickleballuniversity.com/ home/pickleball-warm-ups-and-cool-downs (Accessed: May 2, 2023).*

7. Pickleball University (2023) *Practice prehab and avoid rehab, Pickleball University. Pickleball University. Available at: https://www.pickleballuniv ersity.com/home/prehab-not-rehab (Accessed: May 2, 2023).*

8. Pickleball University (2023) *Step up your pickleball game with these simple stretching techniques!, Pickleball University. Pickleball University. Available at: https://www.pickleballuniversity.com/home/were -not-stretching-the-truth-you-should-stretch-befo*

re-pickleball (Accessed: May 2, 2023).

9. *Rathod, R.by R.R.R. et al. (2023) 10 effective twist exercises for your ABS, STYLECRAZE. Available at: https://www.stylecraze.com/articles/effec tive-twist-exercises-for-your-abs/ (Accessed: May 2, 2023).*

10. *The right way to warm up and cool down (2021) Mayo Clinic. Mayo Foundation for Medical Education and Research. Available at: https://www.mayoclinic.org/healthy-lifestyle/fitne ss/in-depth/exercise/art-20045517#:~:text=A%20 warmup%20gradually%20revs%20up,heart%20 rate%20and%20blood%20pressure. (Accessed: May 2, 2023).*

11. *Sizemore, T. (2020) What you need to know about your pickleball recovery, Pickleball Hut. Available at: https://www.pickleballhut.com/what-you-ne ed-to-know-about-your-pickleball-recovery/ (Accessed: May 2, 2023).*

12. *Spotebi (no date) SPOTEBI. Available at: https://w ww.spotebi.com/ (Accessed: May 2, 2023).*

13. *Team, P.I. (2022) Preparing for pickleball tournaments - mentally and physically, Pickleball Insights. Available at: https://pickleballinsights.com/preparing-mentally -and-physically-for-pickleball-tournaments/*

(Accessed: May 2, 2023).

14. *Warmup before playing pickleball - static1.squarespace.com (no date). Available at: https://static1.squarespace.com/static/543fa8a4e4b 07a3fedf53cf8/t/63dba0288b390d4742c47ccc/1675 337769965/Pickleball+Warm+Ups+Version+1.0.pdf (Accessed: May 2, 2023).*

15. *What exercises build strength for pickleball players? (no date) Paddletek Pickleball. Available at: https://www.paddletek.com/blogs/news/pickle ball-strength-training (Accessed: May 2, 2023).*